RELIGIONS OF HUMANITY

P9-DYP-505

	DATE DUE		

Chelsea House Publishers
1974 Sproul Road, Suite 400
Broomall, PA 19008

The Chelsea House world wide web address is
www.chelseahouse.com

English-language edition
© 2002 by Chelsea House Publishers, a subsidiary
of Haights Cross Communications
All rights reserved.

First Printing

1 3 5 7 9 6 4 2

*Below: An aerial view of the
Al-Kadhmian mosque in Iraq.*

*Opposite: Reading and meditating on a
sacred text inside a wooden mosque on
the Bosporus, Turkey, at the end of the
20th century.*

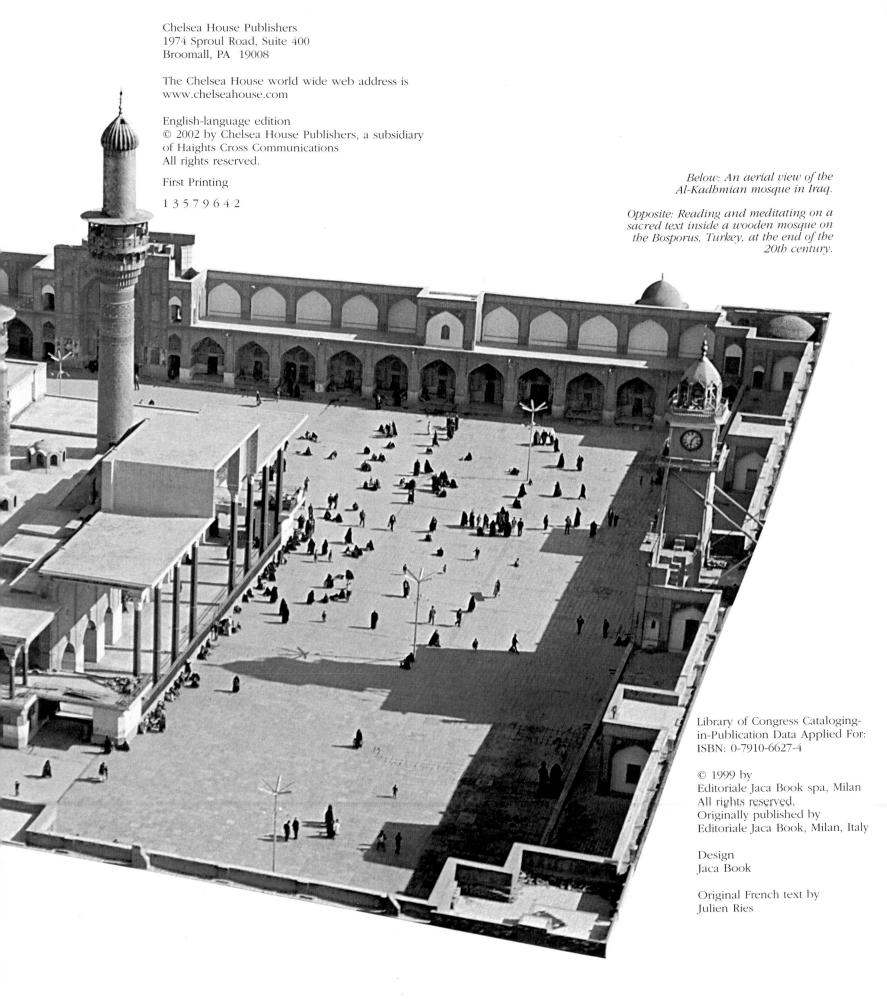

Library of Congress Cataloging-
in-Publication Data Applied For:
ISBN: 0-7910-6627-4

© 1999 by
Editoriale Jaca Book spa, Milan
All rights reserved.
Originally published by
Editoriale Jaca Book, Milan, Italy

Design
Jaca Book

Original French text by
Julien Ries

JULIEN RIES

THE WORLD OF
ISLAM

CHELSEA HOUSE PUBLISHERS
PHILADELPHIA

CONTENTS

Above: A miniature showing an Islamic school taken from an Arab manuscript (the Maqamat of Al-Hariri) of the caliphate of Baghdad conserved in the Bibliothèque Nationale in Paris.

Opposite: A street in Ghardaia, a city in M'zab, in Algeria, a site of great beauty and profound religiosity.

INTRODUCTION

Grounded in fourteen centuries of history, Islam is a religion and a community with an extraordinarily rich cultural heritage, with values and beliefs shared by millions of believers around the world. The religion was founded by Muhammad, an Arab caravan leader and a searcher of God rooted in his native Mecca. An enthusiast and a mystic, he was the bearer of a message resembling Biblical monotheism. Muhammad discovered the one God, the God of Abraham, and he presented himself as the last prophet sent by God to humanity.

Muhammad proclaimed his Revelation to his fellow traders on the caravans, as well as to the merchants and bedouin (roaming desert tribes). He founded his first community at Medina, which served as a model for all future Islamic settlements. By the time of his death, Muhammad's message had already been received and accepted by thousands of believers. In a short time this message was codified in the Koran, to which his companions and friends added the Sunna (or tradition). Over the centuries, the Muslim community has solidified around this message, on which are based all the political, social, and cultural institutions of Islam. Our account will describe the Prophet and prophetism, the Koran and the Sunna, the five pillars, and the one God as the basic elements of Islam.

Muhammad proclaimed the oneness and universality of his faith in the one God. He charged his successors to spread Islam throughout the world, and indeed the history of Muslim conquests and empires bears the marks of the tough origins of this culture, born among Arab caravanists and bedouin. Our account will only touch briefly on these historical aspects.

At its beginning, Islam, like other social movements, found itself touched by violent forces, but it also had cultural and mystic aspirations that would flourish as the belief came into contact with other cultures and peoples. Chapters 9 and 10 will open a perspective on these cultural encounters and on Islamic mysticism.

1
ISLAM AND MUSLIMS TODAY

1

As we enter the twenty-first century, the world's Islamic population numbers around a billion. Of the 180 countries represented in the United Nations, 43 are Muslim and belong to the Organization of the Islamic Conference. As one of the great religions of the world, Islam has produced an impressive civilization as represented by its holy book (the Koran), its mosques, its writing, its literature, and its artistic forms and its traditions. It is a civilization that touches many different peoples, who despite cultural diversities, enmities, and rivalries, share a common denominator: their faith.

The Muslim devotee submits himself to God through the practice of prescribed duties. Such adhesion binds him as a believer before God, and, as a person, unites him with the community (umma).

This act of submission is based on the revelation received and transmitted by the Prophet Muhammad, who, as "the prophet of the last times" and the last prophet to announce the mystery of God the creator and the merciful, also warns the imminence of divine judgment.

The Muslim affirms his faith in the tawhid, the oneness of God, creator and dispenser of all necessary things, Lord of the glory, to whom all praise is due. The signs of God (ayat Allah) provide man with the proof of creation and safeguard his belief, which he professes through the shahada, reinforcing belief in the singular God and in the definitive revelation received by Muhammad.

According to Islamic belief, man is a creature who received his soul through the breath of God and is therefore able to respond to God. On earth he is the khalifa (representative) of God. It is from this relationship that the duties of the 'five pillars' of Islam derive. These cultic practices, when combined with the prescriptions of the community, guarantee adherence to the path toward God as well as harmony within the community (umma).

Thus, the belief in the one God, upon which daily prayer, observance of Ramadan, and the pilgrimage to Mecca (the renewed affirmation of the religion's origins) are based, consitutes the grounding and motivating force that supports modern Islam.

1. *Ablutions constitute a very important part of the rite preceding prayer. These believers are washing themselves in a fountain in one of the pavilions of the Al-Qarawiyyin mosque at Fez in Morocco.*
2. *A school in Baghdad, Iraq in the early seventies. Traditional stories form part of the curriculum together with other subjects.*
3. *Female students entering the great modern university of Baghdad in the early seventies. The university, as if to recall the Abbasid era (8th-13th century) when Baghdad was the leading light of the Arab world and Islam, was meant to express a strong cultural pluralism.*

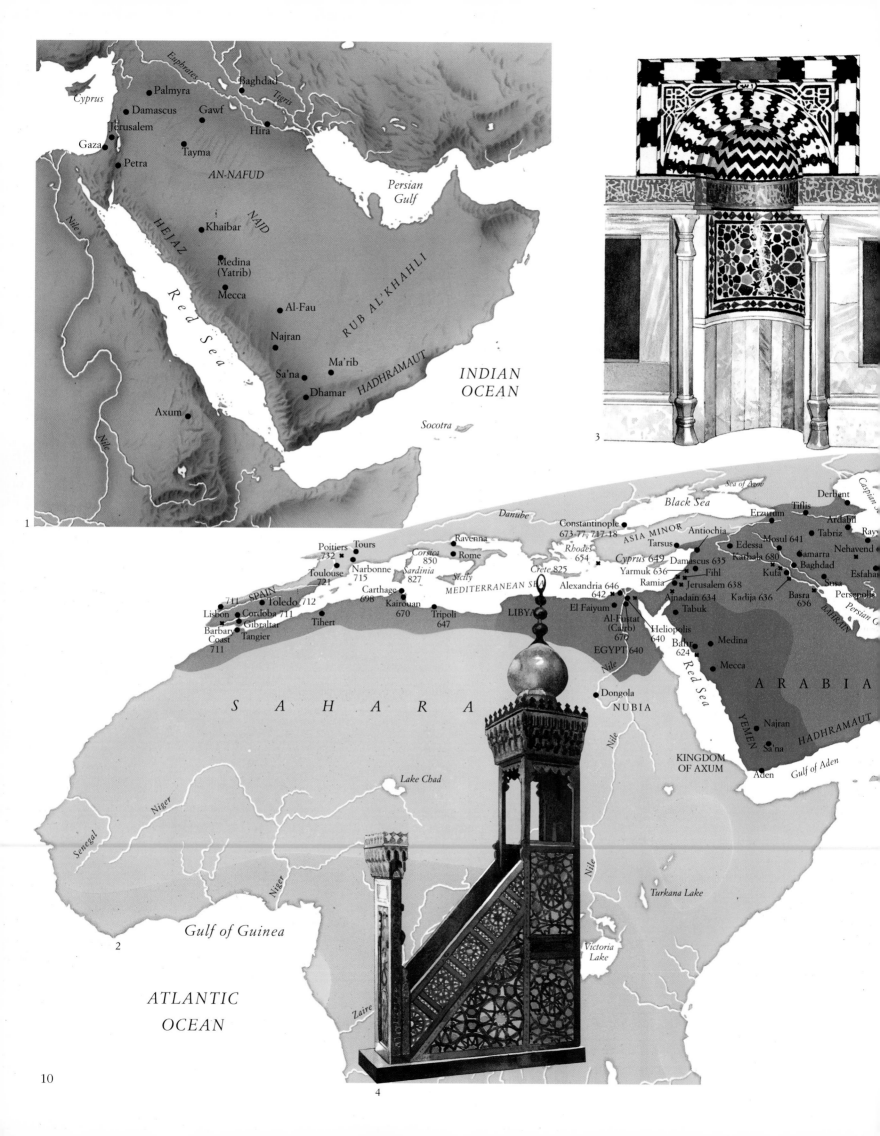

1

Cyprus

Euphrates

Palmyra
Damascus · Baghdad
Gawf
Jerusalem · Hira
Gaza · Tayma
Petra
AN-NAFUD
Tigris
Persian Gulf

Nile

HEJAZ · NAJD
Khaibar

Medina (Yatrib)
Mecca
Al-Fau
Najran
Sa'na · Ma'rib
Dhamar · HADHRAMAUT

RUB AL'KHAHLI

INDIAN OCEAN

Red Sea

Axum

Nile

Socotra

2

Danube · *Black Sea* · *Sea of Azov*

Constantinople
673-77, 717-18 · ASIA MINOR
Ravenna
Rome
Rhodes 654 · Tarsus
Corsica 850 · Antiochia
Poitiers 732 · Tours
Sardinia 827 · *Cyprus* 649 · Damascus 635
Narbonne 715 · Edessa · Mosul 641
Toulouse 721 · *Crete* 825 · Yarmuk 636 · Fihl
Sicily · MEDITERRANEAN SEA · Kufa
SPAIN · Carthage 698 · Alexandria 646 · Ramla · Jerusalem 638
Lisbon · Toledo 712 · Kairouan · 642 · Ajnadain 634
Cordoba 711 · Tihert · 670 · Tripoli 647 · LIBYA · El Faiyum · Tabuk
Gibraltar · 711 · Al-Fustat (Cairo) 670 · Heliopolis 640
Barbary Coast 711 · Tangier · EGYPT 640 · Bahr 624 · Medina
Derbent · Tiflis · Erzurum · Ardabil · Tabriz · Ray · Nehavend
Kathala 680 · Samarra · Baghdad · Esfahan
Basra · Susa · Perse 656
BAHRAIN · Persian G
Mecca
ARABIA
SAHARA
Dongola · NUBIA
Red Sea
YEMEN · Najran · HADHRAMAUT
Lake Chad · Sa'na
KINGDOM OF AXUM
Aden · Gulf of Aden
Niger
Nile
Senegal
Niger
Turkana Lake
Gulf of Guinea
Zaire
Victoria Lake
ATLANTIC OCEAN

3

4

1. *The Arabian peninsula at the time of the birth of Islam and of its first expansion in the seventh century. Consisting mostly of deserts, the peninsula had a number of important cities which marked stopping-places for caravans traveling between Africa, Asia, and the Mediterranean.*

2. *Map showing the spread of Islam from its beginnings to the present. According to the latest available data, 90% of the population in the following countries are Muslims: AFGHANISTAN, ALGERIA, SAUDI ARABIA, BAHRAIN, JORDAN, IRAN, IRAQ, LIBYA, MOROCCO, MAURITANIA, NIGER, OMAN, PAKISTAN, WESTERN SAHARA, SENEGAL, SYRIA, SOMALIA, TUNISIA, TURKEY, YEMEN; 70% in BANGLADESH, EGYPT, GUINEA, INDONESIA, MALI, SUDAN, TURKMENISTAN, UZBEKISTAN; 50% in ALBANIA, KAZAKHISTAN, MALAYSIA (source: Joanne o'Brien, Martin Palmer, Atlas des Religions dans le Monde, Myriad, London/Autrement, Paris, 1994). The map does not show the important Islamic presence in Europe and in its large cities or in North America. The immigration of Muslims*

gives rise to important religious communities and new mosques in the metropolises of the West.

3. *The mihrab of the mosque of the Prophet in Medina, today in Saudi Arabia. The mihrab is found in every mosque and consists of an alcove which indicates the direction (qibla) towards which one has to turn in prayer, that is facing Mecca, the holy city, the destination of the Islamic pilgrimage.*

4. *The minbar in the mosque of Sultan Quasyr in Egypt, built in the second half of the 15th century. The minbar is a sort of pulpit from where the imam calls the faithful.*

5. *Calligraphy, the great art of Islam, creates decorative forms that carry important messages. In this miniature is written the name of God the 'merciful' and the 'compassionate.'*

5

Islam in the time of Muhammad

The conquests of the four caliphs (632-661)

The expansion under the Umayyads (661-750)

The expansion of the Abbasid caliphate (750-c.850)

Islam today

∎ the principal battles of the Arab Conquest

3
THE PROPHET MUHAMMAD
AND THE FOUNDATION OF ISLAM

Born in A.D. 570, Muhammad was a member of the clan of Hashemites, who served as the keepers of the Kaaba, the principal pagan sanctuary of Mecca, and who traded via caravan with Syria. Having lost both his parents at the age of five, Muhammad was entrusted to his uncle, Abu Talib, with whom he later traveled as a guard. At the age of 25 he married Khadija, a rich widow 15 years his senior. Their sons died young, but their daughter Fatima went on to marry Ali, the fourth caliph.

At the age of 40, Muhammad received visions and a revelation (The Koran, 53 and 96), bringing about a profound change in his life. Following this mystic experience, he proclaimed his message, emphasizing the might and goodness of Allah, and the divine justice that will bring either reward or punishment for mankind. From man, God demands submission (*islam*) in the form of adoration, gratitude, faith, and prayer. A number of those who accepted this submission of man (Muslims) congregated around the Prophet, spurring opposition of other clans who realized that the new message would bring about a social revolution. In 619 Khadija died and Muhammad remarried.

Faced with ever-growing opposition (The Koran, 37)

1

2

Muhammad established contact with the oasis of Yathrib, where two Arab tribes and a Jewish tribe had settled. On July 16, 622, the Prophet and his followers left Mecca for this oasis, which was re-named al-Madina (Medina), or 'the city.' This migration, known as the *hegira*, marks the founding act of Islam as a community (*umma*). The *muhajir* is the term for those Muslims who left everything behind to serve God (The Koran, 8).

In Medina Muhammad shaped his community with the first institutions: the organization of the economy and of prayer, the fight for survival, and for the conquest of Mecca. During this time, 74 expeditions were launched against caravans departing from Mecca. On January 11, 630, Muhammad entered Mecca in triumph, destroying idols both in the Kaaba and in private houses, and proclaimed a general amnesty. In doing so, Muhammad became the religious and political head of the new community founded on Allah, the one God.

1. *The mountainous desert landscape of Wadi Ramm in Jordan. Upon these sands trailed caravans on their way to the Mediterranean and the northern Red Sea.*
2. *An illustration from an Iraqi manuscript depicts the Archangel Gabriel who was sent by God to show Muhammad his way to heaven.*
3. *This well-known miniature preserved in Istanbul shows the important meeting between Muhammad and a monotheistic shepherd. The belief in the one God is the basis of the Prophet's message and removes the confusion of polytheism for men.*
4. *The Kaaba, the holy shrine of Islam, is shown in this 18th-century Turkish miniature. It is to be found in Mecca in Saudi Arabia, in the direction of which all Muslims face during prayer.*

4
THE CONQUESTS AND THE EXPANSION OF ISLAM

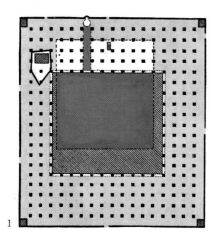

1. Plan of the mosque at Medina. The house of the Prophet in the time of the Umayyads, the first great Arabic-Islamic dynasty, it was transformed into a huge mosque. Muhammad had built the first place of prayer by building a tent on the side of the house.
2. The extraordinary and monumental helical minaret is all that remains, together with the surrounding walls, of the mosque at Samarra in Iraq. A masterpiece of the Abbasid period, it is an almost unique building of its type.

Following a pilgrimage to Mecca in 632, Muhammad died. Abu Bakr (632-634), his father-in-law, was chosen as his successor (caliph). This event marks the beginning of the Islamic conquests in Syria and Persia. In turn, Abu Bakr was succeeded by Omar (634-644), who continued the military campaigns and conquered Damascus in 636, and one year later Jerusalem. An energetic and realistic leader, Omar created military and civil institutions and paid particular attention to the financial organization of the Muslim community. Othman (644-656) collected the recollections of Muhammad and set the official text of the Koran. These three caliphs established the overlordship of the Umayyads, originally an aristocratic clan from Mecca, in the Near East. Ali (656-661), the fourth caliph and son-in-law of the Prophet, however, declared war against the Umayyads. Uniting his followers, the Shiites, he formed a legitimist Islam that demanded fidelity to God in opposition to the dynastic principle, which had become the prerogative of the Umayyads.

The Umayyad dynasty, which had established itself in Damascus first conquered North Africa and then Spain where it had established the caliphate of Cordoba. Damascus, the capital of a powerful state, became the center for the spread of a new culture of Arabization and Islamization. The Shiite Muslims remained opposed to it and on November 28, 749, Abu Abbas was nominated caliph in the mosque at Kufa. The Abbasids (750-945), another hereditary dynasty of caliphs, founded the city of Baghdad, the intellectual capital of the East, serving as a synthesis of the Arabic and the Iranian worlds, and as a great meeting place for the arts and sciences

of the world. In 945 the Turks seized power and the Seljuk Turks ended the Abbasid dynasty. The Shiites, however, continued to rule in Egypt for two centuries, forming the Fatimid dynasty of Cairo.

The Seljuk Turks conquered Anatolia and Syria, where they encountered the crusading armies of the West. These Turks belonged to the Sunni sect, that is, those Muslims who are faithful to the Sunna — 'the tradition.' In their wake followed an invasion by the Mongols, whose leader Tamerlane (1336-1405) later converted to Islam. The Ottoman Turks then set about on their expansion with the fall of Constantinople (1453), the invasion of the Balkans, the conquests of Syria and Egypt, and later of Iraq. With these advances, the Ottoman Empire extended from Vienna to the Nile, from Baghdad to Tunis, and would last for six centuries, marking the beginning of modern Islam.

3. For Muslims, the transmission to the world of the monotheistic faith as taught by Muhammad was felt as duty which was realized by the conquest of various countries. The miniature reproduced here showing Muslim horsemen comes from an Abbasid manuscript preserved in the Bibliothèque Nationale in Paris.

4. Istanbul in the 16th century. Behind the famous wooden houses, there rises the splendid Suleymaniyya mosque, built by Sinan, the most famous architect of the period. Basing himself on the plan of the paleo-Christian Santa Sophia church, he built a mosque with domes, half-domes, and minarets which provide an extraordinary internal light and a fine musicality on the outside.

4

5
THE KORAN, THE SUNNA, AND THE SHARIA

1. A Muslim intent on reading the Koran outside the famous fortified palace of Lahore, in Pakistan.
2. A folio from the Koran showing one of the most ancient Arabic writings known as Kufic. The title of the sura—the Koran is divided into 114 suras—is written in gold. This Koran comes from the great mosque of Qairawan in Tunisia, and is preserved in the National Library of Tunis.

For Muslims, the Koran is the word of God as revealed to and as proclaimed by Muhammad. Supernaturally dictated and recorded by the inspired Prophet, this sacred book consists of 114 *suras* (chapters) and amounts to 6,226 verses called *ayat Allah* — 'the signs of God'. Allah keeps the original containing all revelation: *maktub* — 'that which is written.' Orientalists regard the Koran as a diary of the religious experiences, triumphs, and failures of the Prophet, augmented by a number of ancient pre-Islamic, Jewish, and Christian religious traditions.

The Koran records the primordial pact between Allah and man, which culminates in the covenant with Abraham. Following the death of Muhammad, many versions of his preaching and his deeds circulated among the people, but in 651 Caliph Othman collected all the existing texts and established a single definitive and official Koranic text. Subsequently all the other versions were destroyed.

The deeds, words, and actions of the Prophet constitute a rule of life, practices, and beliefs: this is the Sunna, or the traditions. It follows the path of revelation and serves as a continuation, extension, and explanation of the Koran. To Muslims, Muhammad lived in a habitual prophetic state and therefore all his words, actions, and judgments have a spiritual value similar to that of the Koran. The basis of the Sunna is the *hadith*, a message that can be traced back to Muhammad himself.

The Sharia is the canonical law that includes all the dispositions of God concerning mankind. Deriving from the Koran and the Sunna, it describes the Islamic path for the community (*umma*) and for the faithful. This positive divine law applies to all social, religious, political, and private aspects of life. In the eighth and ninth centuries, Sunnism developed four great juridical schools (*madhhab*) to interpret the law, which remains the fundamental authority. Being of divine origin, the Sharia makes it possible to confront secularization, and gives a religious sense to a daily life steeped in the sacred.

3. *Children from the mountain oasis near Tozeur in Tunisia. The rules of the Sharia are part of the Muslim's daily life and of his entire existence.*
4. *Children beside a fountain used for ablutions near a mosque in Istanbul, Turkey, at the end of the 20th century.*
5. *For centuries Muslims used these portable bookrests to read the Koran.*

3

4

5

6
ALLAH, GOD THE CREATOR, THE JUDGE, THE DISPENSER OF RECOMPENSE

The word Allah derives from the pre-Islamic word *al-Ilah*, meaning 'the God.' Muhammad discovered the one God and proclaimed his oneness (The Koran, 112), affirming Allah as the creator of all things (*al-Khaliq, al-Bari*). In Islam, the creation serves as an affirmation of God's omnipotence and of the necessity for men to discover Allah through the signs of the universe: Abraham was the first to recognize these signs. The creator of man, Allah, will also give him what he deserves on the day of judgment.

Unique and one in Himself, Allah does not reveal his mysterious nature, but may be discovered through his actions which show his onnipotence in daily life. For the believer, Allah is the merciful (*al-Rahman*) and the clement (*al-Rahim*), two names found at the beginning of every sura of the Koran. Guided by a divine hand, it is the duty of humans to recognize God in the order of the world, where 'everything will perish, except Allah' (The Koran, 28, 88).

The perfections of God, understood through the signs and proclaimed in the Koran, lie in his 'divine names.' These 99 names nurture Muslim devotion as believers meditate upon and recite them with the help of a *subha* (rosary). Whole treaties are devoted to enumeration, analysis, and comment upon these 'most beautiful names of God,' which include *al-Malik* (the king), *al-Quddus* (the holy), *al-Salam* (the peace), and *al-Khaliq* (the creator).

Allah dispenses life and death as part of his omnipotence. After death, every human must briefly come back to life for his particular judgment, after which follows the peace of the tomb. There each individual awaits the final resurrection and the universal judgment, during which all actions are weighed by Allah (The Koran, 43, 16-18). The angels will assist Allah in the final judgment, during which all the secrets of the heart will be examined (The Koran, 86, 9). According to the Koran, the faithful and virtuous will then cross the bridge of Sirat (36, 66), which leads from the place of judgment to paradise, while all infidels will fall into hell below. The believers will then enter a garden without parallel, divided into seven layers. This description of the final judgment may have been influenced by beliefs in Syrian Christianity and late Judaism, both of which were known to Muhammad.

1. A tile from a 17th-century Turkish pulpit kept in the Victoria and Albert Museum, London. On it, one of the basic definitions of Islam: 'There is no god except God and Muhammad is his Prophet.'
2. A dialogue between a king and a sage is shown in this miniature from a Persian manuscript conserved in the Bibliothèque Nationale in Paris. Both personages represent a gift and a characteristic which only God can bestow: kingship and wisdom. Wisdom can judge that which is good, while kingship will dispense justice.
3. A lovely Abbasid miniature showing a sermon in a mosque. The imam is sitting on high on a minbar.
4. A fountain in a garden in the great complex of Generalife in Granada in Spain which was the seat of an Islamic Arabic sultanate in the 14th century. The garden with its plants and the playing water represents divine providence: God will provide human life with all its needs.

THE PROPHETS, JESUS CHRIST, MUHAMMAD

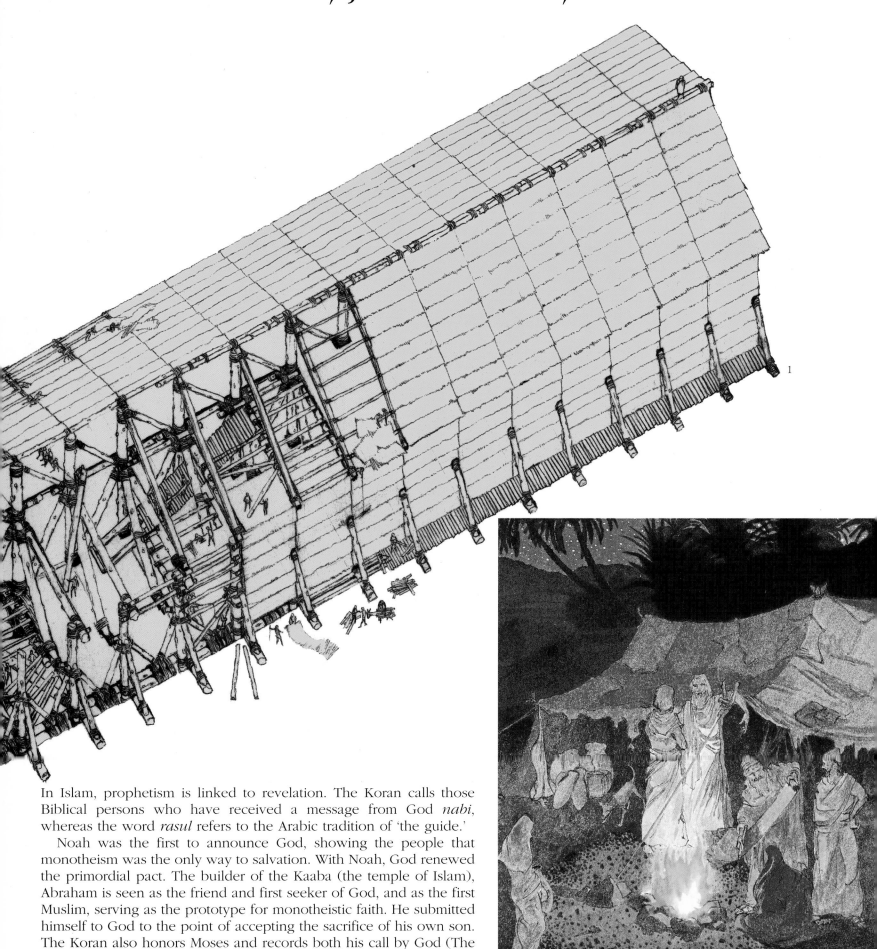

In Islam, prophetism is linked to revelation. The Koran calls those Biblical persons who have received a message from God *nabi*, whereas the word *rasul* refers to the Arabic tradition of 'the guide.'

Noah was the first to announce God, showing the people that monotheism was the only way to salvation. With Noah, God renewed the primordial pact. The builder of the Kaaba (the temple of Islam), Abraham is seen as the friend and first seeker of God, and as the first Muslim, serving as the prototype for monotheistic faith. He submitted himself to God to the point of accepting the sacrifice of his own son. The Koran also honors Moses and records both his call by God (The Koran, 28) and his mission to liberate a people enslaved in Egypt and to spread the message of the one God (The Koran, 20).

In the Koran Jesus Christ is presented as one of the greatest of prophets; he is, however, a man, the son of Mary, a perfect Muslim, and an apostle of Allah. The text of the 15 Koranic chapters mentioning Jesus is clearly taken from the apocryphal gospels. The Koranic text mentions the virgin birth of Jesus, his miracles, his book, and the announcement of a prophet who was to come after him. The Koran calls him the *rasul* of Allah and a *nabi*.

It was Muhammad's duty to announce the pure message of God and to communicate his revelation to all those who already had the Scriptures

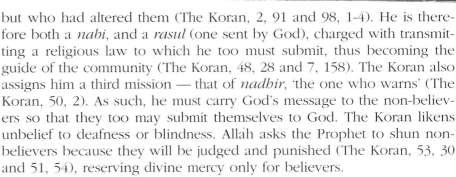

but who had altered them (The Koran, 2, 91 and 98, 1-4). He is therefore both a *nabi*, and a *rasul* (one sent by God), charged with transmitting a religious law to which he too must submit, thus becoming the guide of the community (The Koran, 48, 28 and 7, 158). The Koran also assigns him a third mission — that of *nadhir*, 'the one who warns' (The Koran, 50, 2). As such, he must carry God's message to the non-believers so that they too may submit themselves to God. The Koran likens unbelief to deafness or blindness. Allah asks the Prophet to shun non-believers because they will be judged and punished (The Koran, 53, 30 and 51, 54), reserving divine mercy only for believers.

3

4

THE FIVE PILLARS OF ISLAM

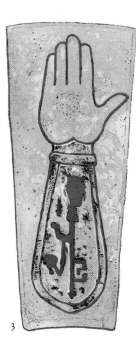

1. *Early morning in the city of Kashgar in the Xinjiang in China. Another day of fasting begins during Ramadan.*

1. The *shahada* is the keystone of Islam—the spoken testimony to the one God (Allah) and His Prophet (Muhammad). Each Muslim must proclaim: 'There is no god except Allah and Muhammad is the messenger of Allah.' It is the profession of the Muslim's faith.

2. Prayer is the expression of the monotheistic faith of man who was created by Allah to serve for His adoration (The Koran, 109 and 110). Personal prayer, the main duty of the Muslim, is thanksgiving to God and memory of Him. The ritual prayer (*salat*), said five times a day, is the liturgy (the divine office preceded by a call, ablutions, and by a proper preparation). If possible, this prayer should be said in a mosque.

3. Alms as required by law purifies the believer, and increases his wealth in this world and in afterlife. *Zakat* is a religious levy paid first at Medina. It is a social institution designed to benefit those in need, the poor, and travelers. The *sadaqa* is voluntary almsgiving offered by Muslims (The Koran, 9, 103).

4. The fast during *Ramadan* (The Koran, 2). Influenced by the Jews and especially by the Christians, Muhammad imposed a daytime fast during the month when he was granted his revelation, the ninth month of the Islamic lunar calendar. The fast must be followed strictly from sunrise to sunset and affects the entire community. The night between the 26th and 27th days is 'the night of destiny' and is spent in the mosque to celebrate the Koran.

5. The pilgrimage, the *haj*, takes the Muslim to Mecca at least once in his life. It is modeled on the pilgrimage of the Prophet himself, taken in the tenth year of the Hegira, in the twelfth month known as *dhu al-hijja*. From start to finish, the pilgrimage is immersed in prayer. Before leaving, each pilgrim

2. *For centuries enormous masses of pilgrims have congregated to the valley outside Mecca in Saudi Arabia.*

reconciles himself with God, his fellow men, and his family. When he arrives at the holy place, he dons a particular garb (*ihram*) and then enters the great mosque. He must then walk seven times around the Kaaba, and run seven times the path of Hagar the slave, to commemorate her search for water for her son Ishmael, the first-born of Abraham. On the ninth day he participates in the catechesis on the plain of Arafat, followed on the tenth day by the sacrifice, which recalls the sacrifice of Abraham. The pilgrimage is meant to heighten solidarity among believers.

3. An engraved stone from the portal of the well-known Alhambra in Granada in Spain. The five fingers of the open hand symbolize the five pillars of Islam.
4. The muezzin, he who calls the faithful to prayer, calls out praise to God at fixed times from the high minaret. The bottom picture shows a minaret inside the Hasan mosque in Cairo in Egypt.
5. A Muslim praying on the bank of Lake Dal in the Indian Kashmir.
6. A 19th-century beggar's bowl from Persia. Many Islamic Sufis (who will be described in Chapter 10) were beggars and they lived on the alms of the other faithful.

ISLAM: SOCIETY AND CULTURE

Islam is a temporal community concerning itself with each believer's relationship with God and also with the relationships between the believers on a moral, social, and political level. Islam has no Church, no priesthood, nor any human embodiment of spiritual power. The Koran is the book containing God's message, but also serves as a code of religious and social life.

The *umma* is the community formed by religious, juridical, and political ties. The *jama* consists of all the believers united in their faith. Personal, family, and social life all assume a sacred character and are oriented toward an effort of expansion of the community in accordance with religious faith as outlined in the Koran.

The successor of Muhammad, the caliph, is a temporal sovereign charged with enforcing the precepts and ideals of the Koran as derived from Allah. These prescriptions concern both religious life and the organization of the Muslim city. Since he has the duty to lead the *umma*, the caliph also has a religious role. Although the *umma* is intended to reflect divine unity, it has assumed various forms throughout history, often endangering this unity. Indeed, after the death of the Prophet, this unity was shattered. The aim of Islam is to restore this ideal community.

Muhammad preached the one God to illiterate bedouin and desert tribes. The transmission of his message provided a foundation for the Arabic writing of the Koran and for all Islamic culture. In the ninth century, scholars in Baghdad translated the great Greek texts into Arabic, marking the beginning of the golden age of Muslim thought. An initially intense flurry of translations was followed by the creation of philosophic, encyclopedic, and historical texts. In the great cities, there arose libraries, storehouses of invaluable treasures devoted to Islamic thought and tradition. Mathematics, the natural sciences, astronomy, geography, and (thanks to hospitals) medicine all underwent notable developments. Islam's artistic contributions to humanity can be seen in a diverse array of cities, including Cordoba, Granada, Mosul, Baghdad, and Palermo.

1. The city of Ghardaia in the north Sahara in Algeria. It looks like a ship in the desert providing succor for the body and the spirit of the traveler.
2. A reconstruction of the Medina in Tunis in Tunisia showing the Arabic city with its great mosque and its intricacy of streets, other mosques, Koranic schools, and marketplaces. The Medina has survived within the modern city of Tunis.

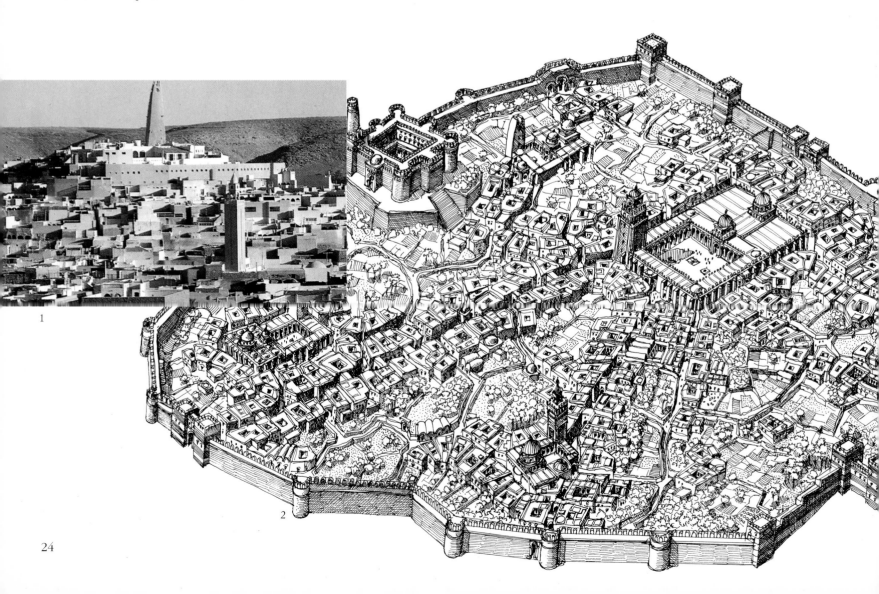

1

2

3. A group of scholars (ulema) is discussing theological, philosophical, and juridical topics in a Koranic school of the Islamic Middle Ages. Below: a celestial globe made in 1050 by the Islamic scientist Ibrahim Ben Sa'id and his son in Spain. The geographical and astronomical sciences were greatly developed thanks to the spread of Islam. **4.** An internal view of the great mosque of Cordoba in Spain (8th and 9th centuries), one of the masterpieces of Islamic art which will exert great architectural influences in later centuries.

10
MUSLIM MYSTICISM: SUFISM

1. The believer prostrates himself during his ritual prayers in the direction (qibla) of Mecca.
2. A prayer hall in the Al Qarawiyyin mosque in Fez in Morocco.

1

3. During the Islamic penetration of India, which took place especially in the cities, the Sufi movement preferred to form small communities in places far away from urban centers. Such communities were dedicated to study and to a religious and ascetic life.

TEXT BY AL-HALLAJ WHICH PROCLAIMS GOD WITHIN MAN

I have a friend whom I visit in my loneliness, a friend present even when invisible. You will never see me listening to Him trying to grab his language from noisy words. His words do not have vowels, nor speech, they are nothing like the melody of voices. It is as if I were a 'thou' being addressed, and were so beyond the thoughts coming to my mind, in my essence, and for itself. Present, absent, near, distant, impervious to descriptions by qualities, He is more profoundly hidden to one's thoughts than profound conscience, more intimate than the flash of thought.

'THE DIWAN OF AL-HALLAJ', QUOTED FROM ROGER ARNALDEZ, *AL-HALLAJ OU LA RELIGION DE LA CROIX*, PLON, PARIS, 1964, PP. 129-130.

The word 'Sufism' is derived from *suf*, meaning 'wool,' and recalls the white woolen habit worn by Christian monks. In Islam, Sufism is the search for God, an example of which is the Prophet in prayer (The Koran, 17, 79). This striving toward the divine continued among some Sufis in Iraq, Syria, Egypt, and the Khorasan into the eighth century. That era in Islamic history can best be illustrated by a woman called Rabiah, who lived a life of prayer and sang the pure love for God. In the ninth century, several schools of Sufism formed and attracted numerous novices. Yet these new institutions faced harsh opposition. In 922 al-Hallaj was crucified in Baghdad for proclaiming that God lives within man. His contribution was decisive for the formation of the Sufi vocabulary.

Following this persecution, Sufism entered a phase during which its elders attempted to reconcile themselves with Muslim orthodoxy. Al-Ghazali, a mystic theologian who died in 1111, stated that there is a proximity between God and man. In Andalusia, Ibn 'Arabi (1165-1240) provided a new impulse for Sufism. A philosopher, theologian, and founder of the doctrine of the 'uniqueness of the being,' Arabi was a renowned visionary, who opened the way for the 'Shiite mysticism of light and fire.' He advanced the idea of a continuous creation, an effusion of the being, through divine compassion, that returns the being to its origins.

From the thirteenth century onward, several mystic movements (*tariqah*, the way) formed around a founder and received the initiatory heritage uniting them with God. Each movement featured a well-defined hierarchical structure, rites of initiation, and practices that furthered each worshipper's search for God. Each brotherhood was marked by complete obedience to the rule, submission to the hierarchy, and secrecy. It is estimated that more than 200 such movements have occurred in total. Sufism has continued to survive and exert influences within these movements.

2

3

GLOSSARY

words in CAPITALS *are cross references*

Abbasids A dynasty of caliphs (132-668 A.H. / A.D. 750-1258) which took its name from its original founder, Abu Abbas. The center of its power was Iran. Abu Abbas founded the capital city of Baghdad on the Euphrates in 183 A.H. / A.D. 803.

al-Hallaj Born in Iran in 858, he meditated on the Koran, interiorizing Islam and discovering the splendor and pure love of God. Stressing God's pact with man, al-Hallaj taught that man is the image of God and that, through love, God becomes present in the mystical man. His preaching began a movement that drew the attention of the political authorities of Baghdad. After nine years of imprisonment he was tortured and executed on March 9, 922. His body was then cast into the Tigris river from atop a minaret. His disciples were persecuted in the hope of destroying the **Sufi** movement, the form of Muslim mysticism which obtains its name from *suf*, 'wool,' the white woolen habit that Muslim mystics adopted from Christian monks.

Allah The one God, lord of all creation, the proper name of God. In pre-Islamic Arabia, the word referred to God the creator among the other gods. The Koran affirms Allah as the one God. There are 99 names of God in the Koran.

Caliph The 'successor' of the one sent by God. The caliph's mission is to continue the political action of the Prophet, the original prophetic mission having been concluded. The role of the caliphate has been profoundly changed over the centuries.

clan A social group that comprises a number of families (decided by maternal or paternal descent) and that serves to pass on Islamic tradition.

Druze A people who inhabit the mountain chains of Lebanon and the Anti-Lebanon, the Damascus region, and the Jabal Hawran massif in south-west Syria. They are descendants from a dissenting sect of the Fatimid Muslims of Egypt, founded in the early eleventh century A.D.

Fatima The daughter of Muhammad and Khadija and the bride of 'Ali, the fourth caliph. She is venerated by the SHI-ITES who call her al-Zahra, 'the resplendent one.'

fiqh The science of Islamic law. *Fiqh* refers to the juridical decisions inferred from the Koran or the SUNNA, with the consensus of the Muslim community.

hadith The traditions that report the deeds and words of Muhammad and, for SHIITES, even those of the IMAM. Various collections of these deeds and words were compiled in the early centuries.

haj The pilgrimage to Mecca, one of the five duties (pillars) of Islam. The great pilgrimage must be carried out during the prescribed month, while the lesser pilgrimage (**umra**) can be performed at any time. The institution of the pilgrimage was initiated by the Prophet.

haram 'forbidden, sacred.' Those places, things, and beings whose free use has been forbidden by divine command are separated from others and are called *haram*. These are the places rendered holy by the divine presence, as well as private property and certain foods. Sacred-*haram* concerns divine presence, while forbidden-*haram* concerns divine commands. The meaning of the word *haram* therefore remains ambivalent.

Hegira 'detachment'. On July 16, 622, Muhammad leaves Mecca and his fellow refugees (**muhajirun**) for Medina. It is the start of the Hegiran lunar calendar in which the year is composed of 12 months with 28 days each. The *hegira* marks the start of the Muslim era.

ijma The consensus of the community, one of the sources of Islamic law, derived from the HADITH of the Prophet: 'my community does not agree on an error.'

imam 'the guide.' He who stands before the believers in the mosque and leads the prayer service. He is also the guide of the community. In SHIISM the *imam* is the spiritual successor of the Prophet, the equivalent of the CALIPH in SUNNISM.

Islam 'abandoning oneself to God, submission to God.' It corresponds to belonging to the Prophet's community, manifested in the cultural and social acts of this religion. Islam is both religion and society.

Islamism The contemporary phenomena and movements of Islamic militancy that began in the nineteenth century to create an UMMA on earth to represent divine unity. The movement gave birth to various revolutionary sects.

jihad 'effort, tension.' The duty of the individual and community to serve Islam. The major *jihad*, or the *jihad* of the bodies, is an action of war to defend or spread the religion. The minor *jihad*, or the *jihad* of the souls, is the forgiving of offenses, conversion by means of persuasion, and one's personal effort to remain faithful to the message of the Koran.

Kaaba The holy shrine of Islam situated at Mecca, rebuilt at the time of Muhammad, a place of symbolic and spiritual reference for all Muslim shrines worldwide, the cosmic pole in the direction of which all Muslims turn during their prayers.

Ottoman The Ottoman empire was founded by Osman the Turk and lasted from 1299 to 1922. Following the conquest of Asia Minor, Eastern Europe, and North Africa, it began its decline in the eighteenth century. After the First World War (1914-1918) only Ottoman Turkey remained.

qibla The direction in which one prays, that is towards the KAABA in Mecca. In the mosque this direction is indicated by the **mihrab**, a shallow alcove in the wall. It is the *qibla* which makes the mosque a cultic place dedicated to God, a holy place.

Ramadan The month of fasting fixed by the Koran and by the HADITH. It is the month of recollection and the slowing-down of activity. The 28-day fast, observed from sunrise to sunset, is an act meant for the community to realize its unity and its mission and to make each adult conscious of being a Muslim.

Seljuks The name of a ruling house of Turkish sultans in Asia, five dynasties of which had great importance in Islamic history. The 'great Seljuks' took Baghdad where they saved SUN-NITE Islam. The Christian crusaders fought with the Seljuks in Asia Minor and Syria.

Sharia 'the way.' It is the path prescribed for believers by Allah to obtain salvation. This law, based on the Koran and the SUNNA, is made up of all the commands of Allah relative to human actions. It includes the cultic, ritual, political, and juridical duties. Both a divine and a human law, it is the model for every generation of Muslims.

Shiism In Arabic *shi'at'Ali* means 'the faction of Ali.' The term refers to fidelity to Ali who was designated by Muhammad as his legitimate successor. In a battle between the legitimists and other factions, Ali emerged victorious and

became the fourth caliph. The Shiite caliph is the expression of the impeccability of the IMAM, recipient of his mission since eternity and seen as the legitimate successor of the Prophet. This legitimism claims to be Islamic orthodoxy. Shiism has experienced great internal divisions. Shiites form the majority of Islamic populations of in Iran, Iraq, Pakistan, and Afghanistan.

Sunna The attachment toward ancestral traditions. This pre-Islamic concept was adopted by the Muslim world, beginning in Medina, where it referred to the actions, deeds, and words of the Prophet. From the early days of Islam, all deeds practiced by the Prophet were considered Sunna. The Sunna has a very precise place in Muslim life: together with the Koran, the holy scriptures, it constitutes the tradition of the Prophet.

Sunnism A current of thought in which the agreement of the community on the person of the caliph guarantees the law. This faction, which is the majority in Islam, started at the beginning of the UMAYYAD empire. The **Sunnis** have remained faithful to tradition and community united in a spirit of moderation, allowing the tolerance and inclusion of a large group of believers. The SELJUK and OTTOMAN Turks, like the Muslim Berbers, have supported the idea of a majority Sunni Islam, as opposed to the SHIITE faction.

tribe A group of clans that share a common language and territory.

Umayyads A dynasty founded by Mu'awiyah in 661, at the end of the reign of the four caliphs. The Umayyads reigned in Damascus from 661 to 744 and in Cordoba in Spain from 756 to 1027.

umma The Muslim community in its religious and political unity. The Prophet saw his *umma* as a unity and as point of reference for all humanity. The community must generate men who believe in God and who live together according to His ideals.

ummat an-nabi The community of the Prophet, made up of all those who wish to live Islam, who profess the Islamic faith, who pray in the direction of Mecca, and who read and meditate upon the Koran. The *ummat an-nabi* is the Islamic institution for all the world.

INDEX